My name is Vanessa Stone, I was raised in a military home with my father who served in the United States Air Force. I was born in Chateauroux, France because my parents travelled with the military to different parts of the world. After my father retired from the Service, we moved to Lubbock Texas where I attended Estacado High School. There I became active in cheerleading, drama and the speech club where I developed my love of speaking, empathy and encouraging others.

As a mother I've always encouraged my two wonderful sons Darrius McCleod and Ernest Wilson to be their best and follow their dreams. I currently live in Austin, Texas with my awesome, loving husband Nolan Stone who has been a blessing to me for 11 years .

I give God all the glory and praise for allowing me to be able to share this book with you, I hope you enjoy this.

I'M HUMAN

WRITTEN BY VANESSA M STONE

ILLUSTRATED BY KARL BAILEY JR

Whether I'm black, white, brown, yellow, green, red, or purple.

2

Whether I have
brown, blue, gray,
green, or black
colored eyes.

I'M
HUMAN

4

Whether I have short, long, curly, straight or no hair.

I'M
HUMAN

Whether I have
long arms,
short arms,
medium arms
or no arms.

I'M
HUMAN

Whether I have
long legs,
short legs,
medium legs
or no legs.

10

Whether I have
a big nose,
a small nose
or a medium nose.

I'M
HUMAN
12

Whether I can see,
or not see.

I'M
HUMAN
14

Whether I'm
happy or sad.

I'M
HUMAN

Whether I
can walk,
ride a bike or
in a wheelchair.

I'M
HUMAN
18

Whether I'm strong
or weak.

19

I'M

HUMAN

Whether I
can talk
or not talk.

I'M
HUMAN
22

Whether you
like me
or not.

I'M
HUMAN

Whether I speak
your language or
a different language.

I'M
HUMAN
26

Because we all breathe the same air and we all have one heart that beats.

I'M
HUMAN

28

We are all human
and we are all
God's gifts.

I'M
HUMAN

Remember to always treat each other with love and kindness.

I'M HUMAN

THE
END